Cloth

by Melanie Mitchell

first step nonfiction

⌐ Lerner Publications Company · Minneapolis

Look at all of the **cloth.**

There are many kinds of cloth.

Cloth is made from thread.

Weaving threads together
makes cloth.

Cotton is a kind of cloth.

Cotton thread comes from cotton plants.

100% COTTON
MADE
IN   Ⓛ
GHANA
SEE CARE ON
REVERSE SIDE

Some clothes are made of
cotton.

Towels are made of cotton.

Wool is another kind of cloth.

Wool thread comes from
sheep hair.

These rugs are made of
wool.

This sweater is made of
wool.

Silk thread comes from silkworms.

These dresses are made of silk.

People use cloth every day.

Cloth is important to us.

Weaving Cloth

Cloth is made when many threads are put together. This is called weaving. Weaving is done by crossing two different threads over and under each other. Weaving has been around for thousands of years. Most weaving is done on looms. A loom is a machine, or frame, that helps people weave cloth. Clothes, rugs, blankets, and many other things can be made on a loom.

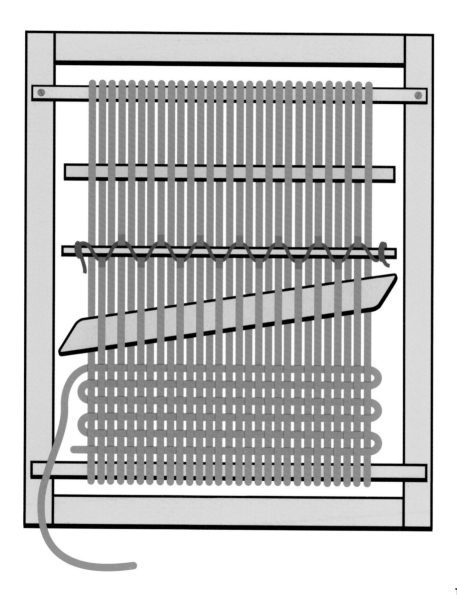

Cloth Facts

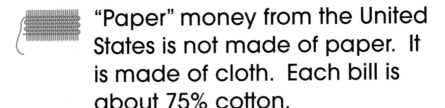 "Paper" money from the United States is not made of paper. It is made of cloth. Each bill is about 75% cotton.

It takes 101 gallons of water to make one pound of cotton or wool cloth.

Australia produces more wool than any other country. It produces 80% of the world's wool. There are about 120 million wool-producing sheep in Australia.

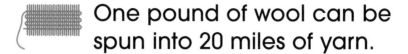

One pound of wool can be spun into 20 miles of yarn.

There are 219 yards of wool yarn inside every baseball.

The outside of a tennis ball is made of wool cloth.

Silk was first made in China thousands of years ago.

Glossary

 cloth – material made by weaving or knitting fibers together

 cotton – cloth made from the fibers of a cotton plant

 silk – cloth made from the fibers produced by silkworms

 weaving – passing threads over and under one another

 wool – cloth made from the soft, thick hair of sheep

Index

The photographs in this book are reproduced through the courtesy of: © Corbis Royalty Free Images, front cover; © Jeff Greenberg/Visuals Unlimited, pp. 2, 12, 22 (top); © Todd Strand/Independent Picture Service, pp. 3, 4, 6, 10, 16, 22 (second from top, bottom); © Norris Blake/Visuals Unlimited, pp. 5, 22 (second from bottom); © Inga Spence/Visuals Unlimited, pp. 7, 14; © Gary W. Carter/Visuals Unlimited, p. 8; © Visuals Unlimited, p. 9; © PhotoDisc Royalty Free, pp. 11; © Erwin C. "Bud" Nielsen/Visuals Unlimited, pp. 13, 15, 22 (middle); © EyeWire Royalty Free, p. 17.

Illustration on page 19 by Laura Westlund.

Lerner Publications Company
A division of Lerner Publishing Group
241 First Avenue North
Minneapolis, MN 55401 U.S.A.

Website address: www.lernerbooks.com

Library of Congress Cataloging-in-Publication Data

Mitchell, Melanie S.
    Cloth / by Melanie Mitchell.
        p.   cm. — (First step nonfiction)
    Summary: An introduction to cloth and its uses in everyday life.
    ISBN: 0–8225–4616–7 (lib. bdg. : alk. paper)
    1. Textile fabrics—Juvenile literature. [1. Textiles.] I. Title. II. Series.
TS1446 .M58 2003
677—dc21   2002006475

Manufactured in the United States of America
1 2 3 4 5 6 – JR – 08 07 06 05 04 03